Making
GODLY
DECISIONS

HOW TO KNOW AND
DO THE WILL OF GOD

Os Hillman

FCP
FAMILY
CHRISTIAN
PRESS

Aslan Group Publishing
3595 Webb Bridge Road
Alpharetta, GA 30005-4140
770-442-1500

Dedication

To Jan Christie and those who are called
to intercede for the body of Christ through prayer.
Thank you, Jan, for your faithful service to me
and the Lord through intercessory prayer.

Acknowledgements

I wish to express special thanks to my editing and team: Charis Hillman, my daughter; Billy Burke, my long-distance editor in Japan; and my wife, Angie, who always gives me important feedback to the content and the presentation. Thanks also to Merriana Branan for assisting with the layout and design.

Bless you all for your valuable input and direction on this project.

Contents

Introduction

Life is filled with life-changing crossroads that result from decisions we are required to make. But how do we know we have made the right decision? Is the decision we make a godly decision? How do we know God is leading us? How do we know it is God speaking and not our own conscience? Can we be assured that we are making the right decision? What happens when you think you have made the right decision and it turns out bad? Is there truly a way to know the will of God and follow it? These are tough questions. But they are important questions that every serious Christian should want to know. My goal in this study is to learn how to make good decisions that are Godly decisions.

A few years ago I went through a difficult time in my life in which I experienced great losses in my business and personal life. These challenges threw me into a search for the whys of my circumstances. I had to know if I was to blame, or if there was something more that I needed to understand in order to avoid some of the events that caused great pain and anguish. Could I have made better choices than I did? Did God simply fail to protect me, or was it all a result of my own poor choices?

My difficult circumstances led me on a journey to seek answers. As I sought answers, God brought people, circumstances, and Biblical truths into my life to give me insight into my situation. I do not feel that I have all the answers. I don't believe any of us will have the complete picture on knowing and doing the will of God until we are in heaven. It is a continual learning process. I, like you, feel that I am still on the journey. I may be a little further down the road than some, and not as far as others. The more I walk down this road of discovery, the more I realize how much I don't know and how much I need to press into the bosom of our Savior to gain more wisdom and understanding in this area.

In 1997 I began writing an internet daily devotional called "Marketplace Meditations," which is now a book entitled *TGIF Today God Is First*. This was a time when I was going through major transitions in my life. God moved me from a career in advertising to a calling to men and women in the workplace. I was, and still am, continually at new crossroads that require life-changing decisions. Because of my devotional, Christians from around the world began sending me questions and dilemmas they faced in their work and personal lives. I found I needed to send them something to help them in their own process of decision-making from a Biblical standpoint. That is another reason for this book.

In this book we will look at the various principles laid out in scripture to make Godly decisions. They will focus on four main areas:

1. Hearing the voice of God,
2. Methods for decision-making,
3. Confirmation processes,
4 . Timing of implementing decisions.

We will provide Biblical examples of these principles as well as personal applications that I have learned from my own experience.

I hope this book will provide some insight into how you can make better decisions in your life. Decisions that will be blessed by God. After all, most of us would rather take the straight and narrow road of life rather than circling the cul-de-sacs repeatedly. I believe this is God's heart as well. I trust this book will provide practical, hands-on applications to help you make wise choices in the decisions you will face in life and work.

1

Vertical Decision-Making

Godly Decision Principle:
Keeping A Vertical Focus With God Insure's Godly Decisions.

Each of us must make decisions every day of our lives. Some of those decisions are simple, and others can be life-changing. A wrong decision can mean the difference between a difficult or easier life. Some decisions will cause us great pain, others will bring us great joy. How can we make decisions that will be the best for us and those around us? How can we make decisions that are Godly decisions?

Well, the good news for each of us is that God has given us a great deal of instruction when it comes to the principles of making Godly decisions. Most of us want to make good decisions, but if we do not know what the Bible says, our good decisions may not necessarily result in Godly decisions.

There are many examples in scripture where men and women made decisions based on presumption. Presumption means that we are overstepping the boundaries and we are presuming something to be true that is not. The principles that we believe apply to a given situation no longer apply because we have misinterpreted or gone beyond the appropriate application.

Keep A Vertical Focus

The number one principle in our efforts to make Godly decisions is to keep a vertical focus on God.

> *I am the vine; you are the branches. If a man remains in me and I in him, he will bear much fruit; apart from me you can do nothing.*　　　　　(John 15:5)

What does it mean to have a vertical focus on God? It means that we so abide in Christ that we are able to hear and do the will of God because of our intimacy with

Him. It means that we follow God's instruction book, the Bible, to make decisions. It means we understand that human logic and reason is not necessarily the method by which decisions were made in the Bible. Having a vertical dimension with God means we don't try to solve problems through our own strength or manipulative capabilities.

The following diagram illustrates this principle.

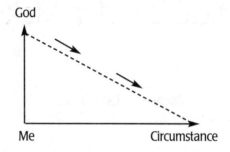

When we have a decision that must be made we have two options. We can seek to decide what is best based on our reasoning (horizontal), or we can seek God (vertical) with a whole heart to hear what He says about the matter. When we apply a vertical focus, God becomes the instrument that will affect our situation. There are a number of ways this process plays out.

During this study we are going to examine a number of ways God provides direction to us, how we can confirm if it is from God, and when we should implement a decision that we believe God has given us.

Following are two examples of those who have gained an understanding of maintaining and applying a vertical focus to making decisions. Our third example describes what can happen when we fail to seek God about a decision and we use our own reasoning.

George Mueller

George Mueller was a pastor in England during the nineteenth century who knew what it meant to live a life that was focused on knowing and doing the will of God. God led him in a walk of faith that has become an incredible testimony to all who hear his story.

Whenever he had a need of any kind, he prayed for the resources and told no one else of his needs. He wanted everyone to know that God answered prayer and could provide for all his needs. During his ministry in Bristol, England, George started the Scriptural Knowledge Institute and built four orphan houses that cared for 2,000 children at the time. When he died at the age of 93, over 10,000 children had been provided for through his orphanages, and he had distributed over eight million dollars that had been given to him in answer to prayer.

How did he know and do the will of God? Henry Blackaby, in his Bible study *Experiencing God*, quotes Mueller on how he kept a vertical dimension with God as he made his decisions.

"...I never remember...a period...that I ever sincerely and patiently sought to know the will of God by the teaching of the Holy Ghost, through the instrumentality of the Word of God, but I have been always directed rightly. But if honesty of heart and uprightness before God were lacking, or if I did not patiently wait upon God for instruction, or if I preferred the counsel of my fellow men to the declarations of the Word of the living God, I made great mistakes." Here is how he summed up the way he entered into a "heart" relationship with God and learned to discern God's voice:

"I seek at the beginning to get my heart into such a state that it has no will of its own in regard to a given matter. Nine-tenths of the trouble with people generally is just here. Nine-tenths of the difficulties are overcome when our hearts are ready to do the knowledge of what His will is.

"Having done this, I do not leave the result to feeling or simple impression. If so, I make myself liable to great delusions.

"I seek the will of the Spirit of God through, or in connection with, the Word of God. The Spirit and the Word must be combined. If I look to the Spirit alone without the Word, I lay myself open to great delusions also. If the Holy Ghost guides us at all, He will do it according to the scriptures and never contrary to them.

"Next, I take into account providential circumstances. These often plainly indicate God's will in connection with His Word and Spirit.

"I ask God in prayer to reveal His will to me aright.

"Thus, (1) through prayer to God, (2) the study of the Word, (3) reflection, I come to a deliberate judgment according to the best of my ability and knowledge, and if my mind is thus at peace, and continues so after two or three more petitions, I proceed accordingly."[1]

David and the Balsam Trees

God describes David as a "man after God's own heart." David learned that he had to keep a very vertical focus in his relationship with God in order to be successful. When he fought against the Philistines he inquired of God as to whether he should attack them. God said, "Yes, I will give you victory." Shortly after this, the Philistines attacked again. This time when David asked if he should fight them, God responded with a slightly different answer. "Yes, go against them, only wait until you hear the marching in the balsam trees" (2 Samuel 5:24). What if David had assumed he should march against them without asking God simply because he had just won a battle? Chances are he would not have gained the victory. Our lesson is that just because we did something one way the first time, doesn't mean we do it the same way the next time. David provides a practical example of our need to depend upon God for every decision we make, even when we have had success in doing it one way in the past.

Avoiding the Gibeonite Ruse

The men of Israel sampled their provisions but did not inquire of the LORD. Then Joshua made a treaty of peace with them to let them live, and the leaders of the assembly ratified it by oath.　　　　　　　　　　　　　(Joshua 9:14, 15)

God's Word also gives us examples of what happens when we lose our vertical focus with Him. When Joshua and the Israelites entered the Promised Land, they fought many battles. In fact, they fought 39 battles in the Promised Land compared to only two in their exodus from Egypt. God instructed them to wipe out all their enemies completely. The more battles they won, the more their reputation preceded them as they entered new territories. Such was the case when Joshua and the people came into the land where the Gibeonites lived. The Gibeonites knew they were as good as dead if they didn't do something; so they dressed up in old, worn clothes and posed as foreigners passing through. They asked Joshua and the people to make a peace treaty with them. An interesting thing happens. The scriptures tell us that Joshua and the people made a treaty with them because they did not inquire of God about these people. They assumed what they said was true. This turned out to be a very bad assumption. They were now forced to abide by this treaty after they discovered their true identity. They got snookered. The Israelites were forced to make the Gibeonites slaves. This created a problem for Joshua and the people, and the reason they got into this problem was that they had started operating on "automatic pilot" and got burned. They had been deceived. That deception resulted because they failed to keep their vertical focus with God. They did not ask God about these people. If they had, what do you think God would have said? However, God did not force Himself on them. He quietly let them fall into the trap. They now had to pay the consequences. Those consequences resulted in having to work hard to avoid cross-tribal marriages while they had to make an entire people their slaves. This was something God never intended them to have to do. The relationship was a source of compromise for the Israelites that made them susceptible to future compromises.

Many of us fall for the Gibeonite Ruse in our lives. It may be a great looking investment. A job that's going to pay more. A relationship that can't miss. Sooner or later we all get entangled in our own Gibeonite Ruse because we fail to inquire of God, or we fail to follow other sound Biblical principles of decision-making.

Therefore, our first principle is to maintain a vertical dimension with God. When we do this, we can expect God to protect us from the "Gibeonite Ruses" of life.

Reflection

1. Would you describe your process for making decisions vertical or horizontal?

2. What protects you from the deceit of your own heart? Have you ever fallen prey to a "Gibeonite Ruse" in your life? Explain. How could you have avoided it?

3. How often would you say you seek counsel from others for the decisions you make?

14

2

The Pro and Con Method of Making Decisions

Godly Decision Principle:

The Bible encourages us to make decisions based on obedience, not outcome.

...Samuel replied: "Does the Lord delight in burnt offerings and sacrifices as much as in obeying the voice of the Lord? To obey is better than sacrifice, and to heed is better than the fat of rams." (1 Samuel 15:22)

After owning and operating an ad agency for almost twenty years, I have discovered that there are by far two primary ways people make decisions today. First, the pro and con method is a system of lining up all the pros on one side, then all the cons on the other side. Whichever makes the most sense is the choice that is made. This makes logical sense to all of us.

The second method of decision-making is based purely on how the decision will affect us, otherwise known as an outcome-based decision. Many of us are guilty of being driven by outcome versus by what is right or by what God is saying. One cannot always determine how something is going to turn out on the front end, and God will not allow a faith decision to be based on perceived outcome. This would cause all of us to make only outcome-based decisions, but sadly, many Christians make such decisions every day. And, I must confess that, as a businessman, I was driven to make decisions that were based on whether I would be financially impacted negatively or positively.

I am not saying that either of these methods does not have a part to play in the process of making a decision, but they should not to be the determining factors. For instance, I recall when my business was going through a lean time. I was losing money every month when I was invited to attend a Christian conference in South Africa.

Logically, it made no sense for me to take ten days out of my month to do this. Also, I didn't have the money to go. However, I felt God wanted me to go, so I trusted Him for the resources. The last day of the registration a man gave me $2,500 to go to this conference. It became a strategic turning point in my spiritual and professional pilgrimage. If I had made my decision based on pros and cons or what I thought the outcome would be, I never would have gone on the trip and I would have missed a huge blessing.

In the early Hebraic church wisdom was gained by obedience. Hebrews learned that wisdom was gained by knowing and doing the will of God and that it often did not line up with logic.

> *The fear of the LORD is the beginning of wisdom; all who follow his precepts have good understanding.* (Psalms 111:10)

However, as the church became impacted by the Greek culture through the influence of scholars like Socrates and Aristotle, knowledge-based systems became more influential in the way education was taught and applied. Greeks believed that the way to gain knowledge was based on reason and analysis.

As a result, the church over the centuries has moved into a more knowledge-based and programmatic system of operation, rather than obedience-based methods that are motivated by a heart fully devoted to following God.

Following are the primary differences between the Hebraic model and the Greek model of learning and applying Biblical knowledge.

HEBRAIC	GREEK
Active – appeals to the heart	*Cognitive* – appeals to the intellect

Distinctives

HEBRAIC	GREEK
◆ Process Focus	◆ Program Focus
◆ Obedience – A Priority	◆ Information – A Priority
◆ Relationships Vital	◆ Controlled Groups Emphasized
◆ Transparency – Love Encouraged	◆ Service – Activity-based
◆ Produces Mature Believers	◆ Produces Shallow Believers

Ultimately, God desires us to take the Hebraic approach when making decisions. He wants us to make decisions based on our heart's desire to follow Him. That means decisions are made based on obedience and there are times when they will not line up with logic. The apostle Paul serves as a great example for us.

Whole-hearted Obedience

In Acts 21, we find an interesting scene involving Paul, the disciples and a prophet named Agabus. It would appear that Paul was going against the Spirit's leading at first glance when we read about the encounter. First, the disciples had a revelation from the Spirit to urge him not to go to Jerusalem. Then, the prophet Agabus actually tied his hands and feet in a prophetic act to dramatize the word of prophecy he was going to give Paul that he would be persecuted in Jerusalem.

> *Finding the disciples there, we stayed with them seven days. Through the Spirit they urged Paul not to go on to Jerusalem. But when our time was up, we left and continued on our way...we reached Caesarea and stayed at the house of Philip the evangelist.... After we had been there a number of days, a prophet named Agabus came down from Judea. Coming over to us, he took Paul's belt, tied his own hands and feet with it and said, "The Holy Spirit says, 'In this way the Jews of Jerusalem will bind the owner of this belt and will hand him over to the Gentiles.'"*
>
> *When we heard this, we and the people there pleaded with Paul not to go up to Jerusalem. Then Paul answered, "Why are you weeping and breaking my heart? I am ready not only to be bound, but also to die in Jerusalem for the name of the Lord Jesus." When he would not be dissuaded, we gave up and said, "The Lord's will be done."* (Acts 21:4-14)

Was Paul acting in disobedience to the counsel of others and even the Holy Spirit's confirmation by other believers? Was the information true? If so, does that mean Paul was not to go? By his response, Paul seems to know something the others don't. He doesn't disagree with the prophecy; he disagrees with the interpretation of what it means. He was not fearful of the outcome of his decision. So often people who have a prophetic gifting deliver a word to an individual and then interpret the meaning and action required. This is not necessarily the role of the prophet. He is the messenger; the recipient needs to determine the action required from the message.

There is no reason to think that Paul went to Jerusalem in violation of the will of God. The prophetic forecasts were not prohibitions from the Holy Spirit but forewarnings of what lay ahead. As a result of these prophecies, Paul's friends tried to dissuade him from risking his life; but the apostle remained steadfast in accomplishing his mission that he believed was from God, in spite of personal danger. The important lesson for us is to understand that doing the will of God does not always have a positive outcome. If it did, we would make decisions based only on perceived outcome. This is not a Biblical way of making decisions. Jesus was obedient to the cross.

Does this mean we are not to make decisions using our intellect? Absolutely not. God gave us the capacity to reason and think. I believe He fully expects us to thoughtfully consider all aspects in the decision-making process. We should research the pros and cons of any decision. Jesus even encourages us to consider all the factors before we take on any new endeavor.

> *Suppose one of you wants to build a tower. Will he not first sit down and estimate the cost to see if he has enough money to complete it? For if he lays the foundation and is not able to finish it, everyone who sees it will ridicule him, saying, "This fellow began to build and was not able to finish."* (Luke 14:28-30)

Fact gathering is an important part of the process for making Godly decisions. Joshua and Caleb were sent out ahead to spy out the land and report back what they found as a form of fact gathering. However, their decision to move forward against the counsel of the others appeared to the others to be an unwise decision. The difference was fear and faith entering into the equation.

Once we gather the facts, the final determining factor on whether we should do something is whether God has directed us to do it, not whether it makes sense.

If the fathers of our faith had made decisions purely based on reason and analysis, do you think Moses would have brought the people to the edge of the Red Sea, or Joshua would have walked around the city of Jericho as a means of winning a battle, or Peter would have paid his taxes from a coin he got from a fish's mouth? I could go on and on with examples of how God confronted the intellect to test obedience. He performed miracles from the most bizarre situations that confronted the logic of His followers.

Partial Obedience

Someone once said that God is a very "pickiune" God. He is very picky. His instructions are to be followed exactly as they are given or we will suffer the consequences. Never is this principle more apparent than in the life of King Saul. Saul's life could best be described as one who was partially obedient. He obeyed God to a degree, but the areas where he disobeyed got him in trouble—even to the point of death.

When Israel appointed Saul as king the people were warned by the prophet Samuel that their nation was to remain a theocracy even though a human king was ruling.

18

*But be sure to fear the LORD and serve him faithfully with all your heart; consider
what great things he has done for you. Yet if you persist in doing evil, both you and
your king will be swept away.*   (1 Samuel 12:24-25)

Saul disobeyed God and His appointed prophet Samuel on three distinct occasions that resulted in negative consequences for Saul and the nation of Israel.

When Saul first became king, he was instructed to wait for Samuel for seven days
after they attacked the Philistines (see 1 Samuel 13:7-14). When Samuel was late, Saul
decided to take things into his own hands and offered a burnt offering in order to gain
God's favor for the coming battle. This was contrary to the instructions given by God
through Samuel, to whom he was to give deference to as his spiritual authority. His
disobedience resulted in a shortened reign for Saul.

The second time Saul disobeyed God was when he was instructed through
Samuel to attack the Amalekites. He was told to destroy everything including the king,
all the animals and other goods. Saul attacked them and destroyed everything except
the king and his choice animals. When God tells Samuel that Saul has committed this
evil, Samuel immediately confront Saul.

*Does the Lord delight in burnt offerings and sacrifices as much as in obeying the
voice of the Lord? To obey is better than the fat of rams. For rebellion is like the sin
of divination, and arrogance like the evil of idolatry. Because you have rejected the
word of the Lord, he has rejected you as king.*   (1 Samuel 15:22-23)

Saul then owns up to his sin and confesses he disobeyed because he was afraid of
the people and gave in to their pressure. It is at this point Saul is rejected as king of
Israel for his disobedience.

When I consider the life of Saul, I realize that I have been like him many times
throughout my Christian life. Saul was a religious man. He had a form of religion. He
was obedient to a point, but it was the follow-through that got him into trouble, and
that difference in complete obedience made God say some very hard things. The Lord
was grieved that He had made Saul king over Israel (1 Samuel 15:35). What horrible
words to hear from God. Imagine if God said that about you or me. This should moti-
vate us to walk in complete obedience that we will never have to hear those words
about ourselves.

Reflection

1. Why do you think Paul was justified in going to Jerusalem when he knew he would only experience persecution? What does the term "partial" obedience mean to you?

2. What were the mistakes King Saul made?

3. Why do you think we can't rely only on reason and analysis to make a decision?

CHAPTER 3

The Dangers of Disobedience

Godly Decision Principle:
If we try to solve problems from a horizontal basis, God cannot help us.

Woe to those who are wise in their own eyes and clever in their own sight.

(Isaiah 5:21)

Many of us have been trained to make decisions and respond to problems in a horizontal way. That is, we often try to fix the problem through our own self-efforts by bringing greater pressure upon it through our reasoning or our natural skills. Perhaps it is a spouse who fails to put their clothes away, or a boss who is overly critical, or a financial problem. God knows the solution to the problem before it ever exists. Our responsibility is to ask God for help in solving the problem and relying on Him to solve it for us. The minute we take on the responsibility, God quietly stands by to let us experience failure until we decide to seek Him for the answer.

One of the best examples of the contrast between a vertical and horizontal dimension in scripture is that of King Saul and David (see 1 Samuel 25). King Saul's mission in life was to kill David. While in pursuit of him there were several occasions when David had the opportunity to kill Saul, but David chose to wait upon God's timing and ways for deliverance because he understood authority. David had such respect for those who had been put in authority by God over him that he would not take matters into his own hands.

Saul represents the exact opposite of this principle. He thought David was the problem and sought to get rid of him through force. As a result, he lost his kingdom because he chose to rule by his own strength instead of living under God's rule in his life.

Another great example of this is Abraham and Sarah, God had promised them a son, but as years passed by they were still without a child. They took their eyes off the One who had made the promise and decided to take matters into their own hands. So, Abraham laid with Sarah's maidservant, Hagar, and she bore Ishmael (see Genesis 16). The son of promise, Isaac, came later, just like God said. However, the modern day conflict between the Arabs and Israelis is the fruit of this act of disobedience that occurred centuries ago.

I recall a time when I launched a business enterprise only to fall on my face. It had all the hallmarks of a Godly venture, but I was premature and guilty of presumption instead of faith. The resulting financial losses are lasting reminders of a decision that was based on a horizontal choice instead of a vertical dependence that required patience until God said, "Go."

These stories illustrate the importance of remaining focused on seeking Him for every detail of life. When we don't, we fall prey to the deceit of our own heart. We move when God never said move. We make decisions based on our own reasoning. The problem many of us fall into is that we don't ask because we are afraid we might get an answer we won't like. It all comes back to that age-old problem of who's going to be in charge. The human heart really would prefer to make its own decisions.

Immutable Laws

There are some immutable laws that relate to decision-making that, if broken, will result in making poor decisions and suffering the consequences of them. These laws, just like the law of gravity, can impact whether you will make decisions that are blessed by God. For instance, if you are trying to make a decision out of wrong motives or a misrepresentation of the facts, you can be sure that God cannot bless that decision. If you have unconfessed sin in your life, you will have difficulty hearing the voice of God and gaining insight through the Holy Spirit's guidance. The scripture says in Romans 8:14 that all who are led by the Spirit are sons of God. Each us should be walking according to the Spirit, not the flesh, so that we can be led to make Godly choices. That is why a vertical relationship with God is so important.

A friend once asked me why a mutual acquaintance did not experience God through answered prayer the way my wife and I did. I happened to know that our friend had held onto bitterness from past hurts in her life for many years. This was the reason this person has made so many poor choices in life and could not experience the power of God. God cannot bless a life that is given over to sin and self-reliance. In fact, I can assure you that if you continue in this direction, God will actually put up walls in order to bring you back to seeking Him in your life.

Reflection

1. When you're faced with a difficult circumstance or decision, do you keep a vertical perspective by seeking God with all your heart? Do you keep a horizontal perspective by focusing on the circumstances and try to figure things out for yourself? Explain.

2. Has God ever made a promise to you that took some time to be fulfilled? If so, did you run ahead and try to make it happen yourself or did you wait?

3. Have you made decisions that were based on wrong motives, misrepresentation of the facts, unconfessed sin or bitterness? If so, what happened?

CHAPTER 4

Hearing and Doing the Will of God

Godly Decision Principle:
*God desires to speak to us personally. Each of us must learn
to discern His voice in order to make Godly decisions.*

Hearing God Speak

Now that we have established the need to make decisions from a vertical relationship with God instead of a horizontal one focused on our circumstance, how do we really operate at the vertical level on a consistent basis? The answer is to develop a heart that can hear and do the will of God.

God speaks to his children in many varied ways. God has said that his ways are not our ways.

> *"For my thoughts are not your thoughts, neither are your ways my ways," declares the LORD. "As the heavens are higher than the earth, so are my ways higher than your ways."* (Isaiah 55:8-9)

If left to reasoning and analysis, we will fail to fully walk in the full counsel of God, which leads to poor decisions. He has also said,

> *The heart is deceitful above all things and beyond cure. Who can understand it?* (Jeremiah 17:9)

Thus, our goal is to avoid being deceived and to develop a listening ear that hears the voice of God with confidence. Our goal is to have such intimacy with God that we can walk in the full blessing of our decisions and to be assured they are not based on our own reasoning alone. Let me reiterate, this does not mean that we do not use the intellectual and logical skills that He has equipped us with. A.W Tozer said that the man or woman who is wholly and joyously surrendered to Christ can't make a wrong choice—any choice will be the right one. J. Oswald Sanders explains his method of receiving guidance from God for decisions; "I try to gather all the information and all the facts that are involved in a decision, and then weigh them up and pray them over in the Lord's presence, and trust the Holy Spirit to sway my mind in the direction of God's will. And God generally guides by presenting reasons to my mind for acting in a certain way."[2]

> *For it is God who works in you to will and to act according to his good purpose.*
> (Philippians 2:13)

God has equipped us with everything we need to make good decisions. Hearing His voice is the first step toward making right choices in life. Now, let's look at the various ways God speaks to us personally and see how they might apply in everyday life.

Here are several ways God communicates with us. We will look at each of these over the course of the next few chapters.

The Bible – *Logos* and *Rhema* Words.
Audible Voice
Intercessory Prayer
Circumstances
Prophecy/other people
Words of Knowledge
Visions and Dreams
Authorities in Our Life
Casting lots

The Bible – Logos and Rhema Word

Logos

> *Your word is a lamp to my feet and a light for my path.*   (Psalm 119:105)

Logos is a Greek word that means "word." It is the literal Word of God. What it says is what it means. God has given us a tremendous resource to find principles that lead to making good decisions in His Word. The first qualification for making a Godly decision is whether or not it lines up with the Word of God.

If you were being interviewed for a job position to manage a company that was involved in illegal activity, that decision would be easy to make. It would not be necessary to spend any time in prayer over that decision. You already know that this would violate a scriptural mandate that requires honesty and integrity in our dealings. Weigh every decision that you make against the Word of God to ensure you don't violate any Biblical principle. God always honors His Word and will never violate it.

Rhema

Rhema is a Greek word that means "living." The Bible is often spoken of as the "Living" Word of God. It means that God will speak to you directly and personally through the scriptures. There have been many times in my life when God gave me specific direction or confirmation of a decision through His *rhema* Word.

Let me give you a couple of illustrations of this principle to help you understand what I mean. My wife, Angie, had only been a Christian for about six months when she began to read the Bible for the first time. She had heard people talk about how God spoke to them through the Bible and she thought they were crazy, until one day it happened to her. She was doing a Bible study and read in Matthew 7 that you could ask and receive. Immediately she thought, "I'll ask God to bring me a husband or someone to fill the gap." The very next verse she went to in her Bible study was "be still and know I am God" (Psalm 46:10). She got a tingle in her tummy and knew that God was speaking directly to her through his "living" Word.

Two years later, the Lord had done a mighty work in her life, and she asked for a husband a second time. Days later, she got a note from someone that had Psalm 27:14 written at the bottom of it. She knew God was answering her prayer for a husband. With great anticipation she opened her Bible only to be greatly disappointed.

"Wait for the Lord, be strong and take heart and wait for the Lord." (Psalm 27:14)

Again, God spoke to her personally through His Word. After that the Lord taught Angie to fall in love with Him, she did not date for seven years until she met me.

Angie views the Bible as God's love letters to us. You can fully expect Him to speak through His living Word regarding a specific situation in which you find yourself. It is one of those mysteries that God does from time to time. As you read your Bible, be aware of the rhema Word of God. He may speak to you in specific ways you never thought possible.

Audible Voice

The watchman opens the gate for him, and the sheep listen to his voice. He calls his own sheep by name and leads them out. When he has brought out all his own, he goes on ahead of them, and his sheep follow him because they know his voice.

(John 10:3-5)

27

A friend of mine told me a story about an experience he had in Israel. They were in the country visiting some of the famous Biblical sites when they saw a group of sheepherders. A shepherd brought his flock and put them in the sheep pen for the night. A few minutes later, another shepherd brought his flock and put them in the same pen. Then, a few minutes later yet another shepherd brought his sheep into the pen. There were three groups of sheep in the same pen with no identifying marks on any of them. My friend wondered how in the world they would separate their sheep the next day.

The next morning one of the shepherds went over to the pen and called out to his sheep. One by one, the sheep filed out to follow him. Only his sheep followed his voice. The same thing happened with the other two shepherds. My friend said it was an amazing scene to watch each of the shepherd's sheep follow him while the others remained in the pen. What a picture of Jesus' words spoken centuries earlier.

What about today? Does God speak to us personally today? If so, how does He speak and how can we be sure it is the voice of God speaking versus our own conscience? Hearing and responding to God's voice is the key to having an intimate relationship with Him. It is the difference between having a religion and a relationship. And it is foundational to making decisions based on a living relationship with a living God. Scriptures record many occurrences when God spoke to His children. From the beginning when Adam and Eve enjoyed unbroken fellowship in the Garden of Eden, we learn that God had intimacy with them that involved a two-way dialogue. Moses provides a great example of the personal relationship between God and man. God was very clear about communicating directly with Moses.

> Then the LORD came down in a pillar of cloud; he stood at the entrance to the Tent and summoned Aaron and Miriam. When both of them stepped forward, he said, "Listen to my words: 'When a prophet of the LORD is among you, I reveal myself to him in visions, I speak to him in dreams. But this is not true of my servant Moses; he is faithful in all my house. With him I speak face to face, clearly and not in riddles; he sees the form of the LORD. Why then were you not afraid to speak against my servant Moses?'" (Numbers 12:5-8)

God speaks through the psalmist to tell us that He indeed will give us direction and instruction. *I will instruct you and teach you in the way you should go; I will counsel you and watch over you* (Psalms 32:8).

There are so many more examples that it would take too much space to recount them.

28

Examples of How God Speaks Today

Yes, God speaks personally to His children. This intrigues me. I have read many books on the many different ways God speaks to people. Many cite that they hear a "still, small voice" and that they have learned to discern when it is God speaking to them.

My good friend, Dr. Victor Eagan, an orthodontist and leader of an international marketplace ministry, tells of his own personal experience in hearing the voice of God.

"I have found that God often speaks personally to me when I am not seeking to hear Him. In other words, I don't often hear Him speak personally when I am having my quiet time of seeking Him. More often it is when I am in my car or in the shower. I know that it is God's voice when the quiet voice inside tells me something I would not normally think to do. For instance, one time God told me to give every one of my employees $1,000. Now, I can assure you that was not my voice speaking. I don't just naturally want to give all of my employees $1,000. However, in this case, I knew it was God and I was obedient," says Dr. Eagan.

I have discovered a pattern in the way God speaks to me when I'm faced with major decisions. I will spend a great deal of time seeking direction from Him and asking Him to speak to me regarding a decision. At some point, I will suddenly get a rush over me with an overwhelming feeling of His presence. The feeling is usually so intense I will begin to cry, sometimes uncontrollably. (Thank God this doesn't happen too often, because it is rather embarrassing in a public setting.) I recall one time when I was praying about whether I should make a commitment to work for a ministry that would involve at least a one-year commitment. It seemed like the right thing, but I was still awaiting confirmation. One morning during my quiet time, the situation I just described came over me. Angie walked into the room to find me sobbing uncontrollably. (She always laughs when this happens and says there's nothing like seeing a grown man cry.) I told her God was telling me to enter into a working relationship with the ministry. It was a great release in my spirit and confirmation of what I was to do. Two years later I was able to look back and see that God had led that decision which resulted in much fruit.

The Muslim Doubter

My sheep listen to my voice; I know them, and they follow me.   (John 10:27)

An Englishman tells a true story of his encounter with a Muslim man as they walked together in the country. The Englishman wanted to share the gospel with him but knew little of his Muslim beliefs. The two men talked as they walked and agreed they would each share their religious beliefs with one another. The Muslim went first and dominated the time of sharing. As he spoke, the Englishman asked the Holy Spirit how to share his faith with him.

"Do you consider your god to be your father who speaks?" asked the Englishman.

"Certainly not," replied the Muslim man.

"That is one of the big differences between your god and my God. I consider my God as my Father who speaks to me personally."

"You cannot prove that," retorted the Muslim man.

The Englishman again prayed to himself, "Lord, how do I prove this to him?"

A few moments later, two young ladies were walking toward them. As they approached, the Englishman spoke to them and made polite conversation. He then said to one woman, "I believe you are a nurse, is that correct?"

Startled, she asked, "How would you know that? I have never met you before."

He replied, "I asked my Father and He told me." The Muslim had his proof. Many of us do not hear God's voice because we do not believe He speaks or desires to speak to us. In order to hear, we must listen. In order to listen, we must believe that He speaks.

In the Pit

"I am in there again," I told Angie, who was not yet my wife at the time.

"And where is that?" she asked.

"The pit," I replied. It was a place where no one could cheer me up, and I wondered if there was a God who spoke personally to me. I needed some direction in my life. God was silent. My finances had dwindled to almost nothing, and I was concerned. I thought it was time to start my ad agency up again or do something to earn some money. Have you ever had times like that? Discouragement can be devastating even to the best of saints. It can bring us so low. The writer of Proverbs phrased it well when he said, *Hope deferred makes the heart sick* (Proverbs 13:12).

"I'm coming over," Angie said.

"Aw, you don't have to do that," I replied.

"I'm coming over. We're going to pray."

About 30 minutes later Angie walked in the door. We sat down on the living room floor and laid on our backs as she began to pray. I didn't feel like praying. I was too deep in the pit. All I could do was listen. We both sat quietly for ten to fifteen minutes, listening for God's voice.

Suddenly Angie sat up excitedly and said, "First Thessalonians 5:24!"

"What verse is that?" I asked.

"I don't know," she said. "That is the verse He spoke to me."

I grabbed my Bible and looked it up. *"The one who calls you is faithful and He will do it."* We laughed. Can God be so personal? Can He care that much? That night God brought me out of the pit and gave me encouragement to be at peace with where I was, and He convinced me that He was a God who speaks.

The Audible Voice

My mother tells of her own personal experience in hearing the audible voice of God. She was at a low point in her life after my father was killed in an airplane crash when I was 14. She cried out to God in her grief and anguish. She was about to have a nervous breakdown. Finally, one night while she was weeping she heard an audible voice, "Trust me, Lillian." That is all it was and that is the only time she has ever heard an audible voice, but it has been the one thing that has kept her for more that 35 years.

I have had the privilege of hearing testimonies of some Christians in Muslim countries. There have been many instances in which God has appeared and spoken to Muslims in Saudi Arabia and other such nations.

Reflection

1. How often would you say you spend reading the Bible? God can't effectively speak to us if we don't have His Word hidden in our hearts.

2. Has there ever been a time when you felt God spoke to you through the *rhema* Word of God? Explain.

3. God desires to speak to you personally. What changes might be necessary in your life to be able to listen better?

5

How God Speaks to Us Through Others

Godly Principle:
God uses multiple ways of communicating to His children.

For the next few chapters we want to review how God speaks to us. It is remarkable the different ways God chooses to speak to His children in order to provide direction. One of the major ways God speaks is through other Christians. He gives his children different gifts in the body of Christ that allow Him to speak to us. Paul describes several of these spiritual gifts in Romans 12 and 1 Corinthians 12 and 14.

Intercessory Prayer

> *Epaphras, who is one of you and a servant of Christ Jesus, sends greetings. He is always wrestling in prayer for you, that you may stand firm in all the will of God, mature and fully assure.* (Colossians 4:12)

When God began to bring me into a greater depth of understanding of His ways, one of the areas He began to teach me about was intercessory prayer. When I speak of "intercessory prayer," I speak not just of prayer but of prayer that intercedes for some one or for some thing. It is prayer that seeks to enter into a deeper level of intimacy and hearing from God. My first encounter with this was when I was going through the major part of my crisis. I was out of town when a major ministry published a story about me. An intercessor named Jan Christie called to learn more about my work. Surprised to learn I lived in the same area as she did, she came by our office and met with a woman on our staff. Jan asked if they could spend time praying together. She knew little of me or anyone else in my office and yet when she began praying she said she saw a picture of three men and began to describe each one in detail. At the conclusion of her prayer our staff person said, "You just described the three men in our office." That was the beginning of my introduction to an "intercessor."

Jan has since become my intercessory prayer director and is now a vital part of the ministry God has called me to in the workplace.

What is intercessory prayer? It is simply one who intercedes for others (Ephesians 6:18; Colossians 4:12). *Webster's New World Dictionary* defines "intercedes" as to plead or make a request on behalf of another or others. It is a priestly calling of all believers (1 Peter 2:5; Exodus 19:6), and it is the Holy Spirit praying in us (Romans 8:26, 27). Intercession is not a spiritual gift but a calling for each believer. However, some people are called to greater degrees of intercession and often appropriate the gift of prophecy as well. We must realize that if we are truly in a spiritual battle; then, we must engage those in the body who are front-line scouts who can warn us against impending attacks and minefields. Intercessors are those people.

A few years ago I was on a trip to meet with some partners on a ministry venture. For months I had been troubled about the direction the venture was taking. However, I had not been able to clearly discern whether my issue was "my issue" or something that God wanted addressed. I had not shared this with Jan but had asked her simply to pray about something I was concerned about. The concern I had related to a very "foundational issue" within the ministry. The next morning I checked my e-mail and Jan had sent me a note that said she was praying and God seemed to impress her to encourage me to address boldly anything that was on my heart, especially anything that was "foundational." She actually used those words. This was confirmation for me to know that what I was sensing was from God. This gave me boldness to address my concern.

It should be noted that intercessors are not there for us to gain direction from God. They are there to help us discern danger and confirm direction. Someone once described them as scouts in a battalion. They seek to discern where the minefields of danger are and report back to the generals. It is always a safe policy to get confirmation from several sources before you move in a direction. God is bringing more and more light to the area of intercessory prayer and how it can be integrated into our personal and work lives. I personally know of several businesses who have made a commitment to add or develop intercessory prayer as a vital part of their business.

Five Points

The last several years I have come to know some incredible men and women of God. One such friend is Emeka Nwankpa from Nigeria. Emeka has been trained as a barrister in the nation of Nigeria. However, in the last several years God has trained him as an intercessor, and is director of intercession for the International Christian Chamber of Commerce, and has directed intercessory prayer for the nation of Nigeria. He shared this amazing story at our second Marketplace Leaders Summit a few years ago.

"I had to handle a case on appeal. In preparing for that case, I had written out a brief for five grounds of appeal. I had prayed. My wife had prayed. My junior in chambers had prayed. That morning I came into court. I tried to talk to some of the senior members of the bar to see if they could give me any tips. Because this legislation was very new at the time, the case law on it was very little. It had not been recorded for people to get out of law reports. So here I am in court and I bow my head and I begin to pray. And the Spirit of God told me, 'Cancel grounds one through four, argue ground five.'"

"Since it was me who was to start, the judge said, 'Well, proceed.'"

"'Your Lordship, I first want to inform the court that I wish to withdraw grounds one through four.'"

"'Counsel, are you sure you want to do this?'"

"'Yes, your Lordship.'"

"'Well, grounds one through four are struck out. Proceed on ground five,' said the judge.

"I finished my argument on ground five and I sat down. The lawyer on the other side got up and for twelve minutes could not get a word out of his mouth! He opened it, closed it, turned this way, then that way, and he stammered; then he finally said, 'It is unfortunate that my learned friend has withdrawn grounds one to four.'

"He sat down and resigned the case. I found out later he had prepared grounds one to four and had nothing for ground five, so, you know who won the case."

Fasting/Prophecy/Words of Knowledge

While they were worshiping the Lord and fasting, the Holy Spirit said, "Set apart for me Barnabas and Saul for the work to which I have called them." So, after they had fasted and prayed, they placed their hands on them and sent them off.

(Acts 13:2-3)

There are times in our lives when major decisions require a concerted effort to press into the heart of God. God has gifted some in the body of Christ to have special gifts in the area of intercessory prayer, prophecy, and even words of knowledge about specific situations (see 2 Corinthians 14). In Acts, chapter 13 we find a situation in which the disciples were worshiping and fasting. During this time God spoke to them with some specific instructions. It was a strategic time in the church in which Barnabas and Saul were set apart for the work God had called them. Fasting was an important aspect of hearing from God.

Angie and I often set aside a time of fasting and prayer whenever a major decision needs to be made. Fasting is a physical demonstration to God that we are serious about wanting an answer. It allows us to be totally focused on the issue at hand. The physical aspects of fasting contribute to our mind being more in tune with the spiritual dimensions of life. In 1997, I was troubled over where I was in my life. It seemed nothing was moving forward. I was struggling with whether to rebuild my advertising agency or focus on the new calling God seemed to be raising up. I assumed my fast would be a few days. However, as each day went by I did not feel I was getting direction. I extended it for a few more days. By the time I was on my fourteenth day, I decided to fast for forty days. It just so happened that the last day of my fast was the first day of a conference I had planned to attend months earlier. That night an intercessor name Bradley Stuart from South Africa came forward with a word of prophecy for someone in the audience. It was a small group of less than 50 people in attendance. The minute he read his words I knew they were directed at me because the scripture verse he used had been a passage that God has used consistently in my life during my journey. Besides, I had already had a similar message given to me thirty days earlier by another friend. Here is the message the Lord gave him.

"The past few years have been times of deep preparation where I have allowed you and your business to be torn and smitten. But this is the season where I want to start to restore and heal you. However, right now, as you are about to be restored it is a time when I want you to allow me to show you what I have been teaching you. The seed is about to spring forth so simply wait and rest in me. I am in control, I am working on the seed and it shall come forth as I send the gentle rains."

And they will seek my face; in their misery they will earnestly seek me. Come, let us return to the LORD. He has torn us to pieces but he will heal us; he has injured us but he will bind up our wounds. After two days he will revive us; on the third day he will restore us, that we may live in his presence. Let us acknowledge the LORD; let us press on to acknowledge him. As surely as the sun rises, he will appear; he will come to us like the winter rains, like the spring rains that water the earth.

(Hosea 5:15- 6:3)

This was a strategic time in my life when God used this intercessor to confirm His direction in my life. I sensed this was a confirmation because of the direct relationship it seemed to have from a message I received only a few weeks earlier from a friend in another state. Notice the similarities between the two messages.

"I believe that God is saying that the worst is over for you and that you need not fear any repeat of the pain of the past. You are not a second rate son as the enemy of your soul will try to tell you. Lift up your eyes and see your Father smiling at you. From now on, you will work with God, rather than just for Him. He will show you the plan and the steps. You have learned to wait for His voice. There is a latter rain for your life. It will refresh you and cause you to forget the dryness of the past. Even now, the clouds are forming. There will be new crops, new fields, new harvests, new plantings, new partners in your life."

This message was also another confirmation to me about Angie, who represented a "new planting and new partner" in life who I would marry eight months later.

Prophecy and Words of Knowledge

Timothy, my son, I give you this instruction in keeping with the prophecies once made about you, so that by following them you may fight the good fight, holding on to faith and a good conscience. (1 Timothy 1:18-19)

Perhaps you are reading this now and cannot identify with me because you have never had any experience with gifts of prophecy or words of knowledge. I, too, came from a background that did not expose me to this area of ministry. However, God has brought people into my life that clearly operate in these gifts, and I have seen them valuable to affirm Christians in their faith. Prophecy tends to reveal information about your past or future and is used to encourage you in your faith. Words of knowledge tend to provide information about a particular situation.

God can often use other individuals to convey His plans and direction for your life. It does not have to be couched in religious language like "prophecy" or "words of knowledge." It may come in a simple conversation with another person. A word might be communicated that sparks a cord in your spirit. Perhaps a person confirms something you have heard from someone else. Be aware of these types of situations. God is using them to communicate important information to you and to provide direction in your decision-making process.

Called to the Mission Field

When Angie and I met for the first time, she told me she was called to the mission field. The moment she said that I heard the words in my inner spirit "she is called to the mission field but it is not what she thinks." I did not totally understand what that meant; I just knew they were not my thoughts. I did not share these thoughts with her. However, the following week we were together and she asked if I would pray for her. She revealed that she thought she was supposed to go the mission field but was unsure where she was to go. I then felt I was to share that I heard the words that "she was called to the mission field but it's not what she thinks." She actually got rather angry with me because she thought I was simply trying to date her. A year and a half later we were married and she agrees that she is called to the mission field, but it definitely is not what she thought. She is called to a workplace mission field with me and we are traveling overseas together quite often. This was a word of knowledge that God gave me for Angie about her particular situation.

Visions and Dreams

During the night Paul had a vision of a man of Macedonia standing and begging him, "Come over to Macedonia and help us." After Paul had seen the vision, we got ready at once to leave for Macedonia, concluding that God had called us to preach the gospel to them. (Acts 16:8-10)

The apostle Paul had many dreams and visions that provided direction for his ministry. God can use dreams to give us specific direction or revelation about something in our lives. Six months into the major crisis I went through, I awoke in the middle of the night during a dream. The dream was short but very detailed. It showed me looking over my shoulder into a large gathering of people. I was speaking to those people about God. That was all there was to the dream. At the time the dream seemed ridiculous, given my situation. I never really thought much about that dream until I began speaking to groups as a result of the marketplace ministry in which I have been involved. I believe God was giving me a snapshot of the future.

The first time I met with my intercessory prayer director we were praying together in a restaurant. At the conclusion she shared a vision of myself standing in front of a crowd of people speaking. It was the very same dream.

Peter's Vision

While Peter was wondering about the meaning of the vision, the men sent by Cornelius found out where Simon's house was and stopped at the gate. They called out, asking if Simon who was known as Peter was staying there. (Acts 10:17-18)

In Acts 10 we find a situation in which Peter has a vision that encourages him to visit a man named Cornelius, who is a gentile centurion. Peter had refused to associate with gentiles and felt the gospel was for the Jews only, but God showed him in a dream that this was not so, and that he was to go speak with Cornelius. At the same time, God sent an angel to Cornelius and told him to go get Peter and invite him to his house. What a neat story of God orchestrating events through dreams and visions.

A Vision of Trees

On three different occasions I have had three different people from three different regions of the world describe a vision during a prayer time we were having that described my life as a tree. Each vision, in a progressive way, had one additional detail the previous one did not have. The last one of these was when I was on the island of Cyprus and a man from England shared this vision during a prayer time with me. The visions have been strategic confirmations of God's path for me.

Out of the Mouth of Babes

One Friday night we had our niece and nephew over to spend the night. Our 5-year-old nephew awoke the next morning and told Angie he had had a dream that our house had been run over by a bulldozer. When Angie told me this we looked at each other in amazement. A few months earlier, we had signed a contract to sell our home and property to a commercial development company that was going to clear off our land for a housing development. The child was not aware of these plans.

Reflection

1. God speaks through many different ways. Have you ever fasted before making a major decision. Consider fasting the next time you must make a major decision.

2. Sometimes God uses others to speak into our lives. Be aware of times when somebody might say something that relates to a major decision that you are about to make. It may be God speaking through that person.

3. Has God ever spoken to you through a prophecy or word of knowledge? Explain.

6

How God Speaks to Us Through Authority

Godly Decision Principle:
God often uses authority structures to guide us in our decisions.

Authority and the Will of God

Obey your leaders and submit to their authority. They keep watch over you as men who must give an account. Obey them so that their work will be a joy, not a burden, for that would be of no advantage to you. (Hebrews 13:17)

Man's very first sin was disobedience in the Garden of Eden when Eve believed the serpent's promise that if she ate from the fruit tree in the middle of the garden she would be like God. Eve fell for Satan's lie, and Adam was also deceived into going along with the idea. This was man's first bad decision that led to consequences that have affected mankind until even today. What was the real sin here? God had laid one ground rule in the Garden in order to protect Adam and Eve. God was their one authority structure that they were supposed to live under in order to have His protection. Adam and Eve's sin was an act of rebellion and disobedience against His authority because they wanted something more. It was the serpent who encouraged them to seek more. Satan made the offer look so good that Eve could not resist.

This same scene takes place every day. We are propositioned by circumstances that appear on the surface to give us a better life, increase our knowledge and pleasure, and make us "gods." They are often presented in neat, professional packages that don't have the appearance of evil. Ultimately the result, if Satan is successful in deceiving us, is unprotection and death...separation from the path God has planned for us. This sends us down detours in life that have many harmful consequences.

As a business owner for over fifteen years, I made many decisions that I regretted because I didn't understand the Biblical truths of authority, accountability, and mutual submission. I have found many other business people in the same state of ignorance. God's Word says much about protecting His children from harmful actions if they will follow some simple guidelines found in scripture. When we violate His truth, we open ourselves up to the deceit of our own heart resulting in making wrong decisions.

I always viewed the term "authority" to mean someone I must submit to whether I liked it or not. It was a negative, restrictive term in my mind. There was nothing positive about the concept. I realized I had not been exposed to many authority structures in my own life. A friend helped me understand that this was a major void in my life. I lost my father when I was fourteen in an airplane crash. I grew up making many of my own decisions after that. I decided where to go to college, where I would live, and what jobs I would take. I decided when I would start my own company. I made all the major life decisions with little input from others.

> *Everyone must submit himself to the governing authorities, for there is no authority except that which God has established. The authorities that exist have been established by God.* (Romans 13:1)

After I became a Christian, I sought God in those decisions, but I had never been accountable to anyone else for my decisions. As a business owner, I made some poor decisions due to a lack of accountability. I didn't know they were poor at the time, but the results proved that they were. Many times they affected employees, my wife, or even my child. What I have come to realize now is that God has given each of us people in authority over us to help us avoid the pitfalls of wrong decisions. This is the government of God. It is one of His structures for insuring Godly decisions and protecting us from unnecessary pain due to making the wrong decisions. Protection is the key word when we begin looking at the word "authority." That is the purpose for God's authority structures.

Five Key Authority Structures

All of us have a multitude of character weaknesses that need to be perfected. God uses those in authority over us to perfect these character flaws. We find these authorities in five main areas: family, church, business, government, and personal relationships. God has set up His plan for relationships and human development within a structure of authority to accomplish three major purposes in our lives:

1. To grow in wisdom and character and ultimately to become more Christlike.
2. To gain protection from destructive and deceptive temptations.

3. To receive clear direction and confirmation for life decisions.

God wanted authority structures in our lives to accomplish several needed things important to every believer.

Let every person be in subjection to the governing authorities. For there is no authority except from God, and those which exist are established by God. Therefore he who resists authority has opposed the ordinance of God; and they who have opposed will receive condemnation upon themselves. For rulers are not a cause of fear for good behavior, but for evil. Do you want to have no fear of authority? Do what is good, and you will have praise from the same. (Romans 13:1-3)

God requires us to honor those who are in authority over us. These include government authorities as well as those over us in our families, work, church body, and personal relationships. It does not say we must agree with them or even socialize with them. It simply says we are to respect them as authorities that God has placed over us. We are to give them deference. When we dishonor those in authority, we dishonor God. We will receive condemnation upon ourselves if we follow this path.

Five Key Authority Structures

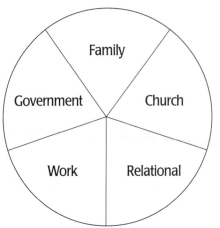

Accountability in Marriage

Submit to one another out of reverence for Christ. (Ephesians 5:21)

We have an identity crisis in the family when it comes to Biblical roles and authority. It seems everything is messed up. Women have been deceived to believe that

43

Biblical submission equals slavery and unequalness. Men use this concept to manipulate and control. Neither is what God had in mind. Today, even children have become the leaders in the home due to the insecurities of many parents who want only the best for their children at any cost.

Authority is simply delegated responsibility. The Bible teaches that the husband is the head of the home (Ephesians 5:23). God doesn't say he is smarter, more capable, or deserving. It's the way God set things up in His design of the family. The emphasis is not on who's the boss, but on who is ultimately responsible. Headship in the home is the man taking loving responsibility for the condition of his family. No man will have peace in his home if he views authority as simply the domination of his wife and children. God wants couples to make decisions together, each drawing upon the wisdom of the other, and enjoying themselves as friends in open and loving communion.

Parental Authority

Another authority is our parents. If we are still single, our parents are the primary authority relationship God has placed over us to provide direction in our lives. When we marry we still have a responsibility to honor our parents, but scripture clearly teaches we are to leave and cleave to our mates. God has many things to say regarding honoring our parents.

> Honor your father and your mother, so that you may live long in the land the Lord your God is giving you. (Exodus 20:12)

If we do not honor our father and mother, we are susceptible to a short life. In the Old Testament the importance of honoring father and mother was extremely important. The penalty for not doing so was death.

> And he who strikes his father or mother shall surely be put to death. (Exodus 21:15)

> And he who curses his father or his mother shall surely be put to death. (Exodus 21:17)

> If a man curses his father or mother, his lamp will be snuffed out in pitch darkness. (Proverbs 20:20)

God placed a very high priority on respecting parents. Whatever our age, we are instructed to always be responsive to our parent's counsel:

> Listen to your father, who gave you life, and do not despise your mother when she is old. (Proverbs 23:22)

44

It is the "office" that our parents hold that God wants respected. He is very aware of their shortcomings. God placed those parents in our lives to allow us to develop certain character qualities. We can choose not to have ongoing fellowship with a parent whose behavior is viewed as destructive, but we still must honor the office they hold. That is the distinction.

I once asked my twelve-year old daughter, "Do I have a right to ask you to do something that you don't want to do?" She answered yes. Then, I asked her to do something that I knew was going to be difficult, yet I also knew the request was legitimate. She didn't agree and began to cry and said that her feelings told her that she could not do what I asked her to do. Where did that leave me? I was left with a daughter who can now decide when she can say no to her father if her feelings don't line up with the request. This was an issue I had to stand firm on and would not yield. I reviewed with her that our family would uphold a standard of behavior and that I would not accept anything less. I told her that there are situations which make it appropriate to disobey an instruction from one of her parents. I explained that if I ever told her to do something that was unscriptural, then this was cause for disobedience. This would hold true in a job situation or governmental law. God's law is always higher than man's law.

Children have often become the leaders in many homes today. Satisfying their desires and trying to make them happy has become too much the norm, even in the church. When we fail to provide Biblical leadership in the home, we fail to provide the proper "fences" that are designed to let our children know their boundaries. If those boundaries are not respected, they will be subject to Satan's attack because they no longer are living under the protection of their God-given authority. This concept is being lost in our American culture, and we are seeing the catastrophic results of it in the increasing numbers of teen pregnancies, crime in schools, and lower academic scores.

Confirmation Through a Parent

When Angie and I decided to get married, she was 36-years-old and I was 45. Angie had never been married and had learned that her father was still her authority figure for giving direction in her life. She also did not equate his spirituality with God's ability to provide direction for her. God used his counsel at different times in her life, even though he often did not realize how God was using him. Again, we must realize authority figures in our lives represent "offices" through which God works and are not based on their qualifications necessarily to give input. It is a faith decision to seek counsel through God's authority figures in our lives.

My finances were not very secure when I asked Angie to marry me, and I had more debt than she had ever seen. She wanted to review my finances with her father before agreeing to a wedding date. I feared that he might dissuade us based on this situation. We met with him and I reviewed my finances and overall situation. To my surprise, he gave us his full blessing. This gave Angie a real peace that her dad was providing yet another confirmation of our relationship.

Authority in the Workplace

If we work for someone, we must recognize that they are placed in authority by God.

> *Slaves, be obedient to those who are your masters according to the flesh, with fear and trembling, in the sincerity of your heart, as to Christ: not by way of eyeservice, as menpleasers, but as slaves of Christ, doing the will of God from the heart. With good will render service, as to the Lord, and not to men, knowing that whatever good thing each one does, this he will receive back from the Lord, whether slave or free.* (Ephesians 6:5-8 See also Colossians 3:22, 24;*
> *1 Peter 2:18; 1 Timothy 6:1, 2)*

We had several instances in our business where we had to deal with insubordination within our company. This had to be dealt with directly with the individual. In one instance, we had to release an employee because of unwillingness to live under the same policies established for all of our staff. As a Christian-owned company, we believed Biblical principles should apply to our business.

There are a variety of authority and accountability structures in business that differ in their level of authority. In a corporation the board of directors has absolute authority to implement changes within the corporation. They are fiscally responsible for the actions they take on behalf of that corporation, whether it is a for-profit business or a non-profit organization Those who operate under the leadership of the board are under their authority. The board of directors are there to make decisions for the corporation.

This is not the case for a Council of Advisors in a privately held company. An advisor's role is to offer suggestions, alternatives, and options. It is not to make decisions for the CEO of the company. The ultimate responsibility for making those final decisions still rests with the CEO because he is the one that is responsible for the impact of those decisions, not the advisors. If the advisors made a decision that left the company bankrupt, the advisors would not be liable for debts, the CEO would be. The Council of Advisors brings Godly advice, counsel, prayer, perspective, encouragement, accountability, and protection to the CEO of the company. The advisors should be people in whom the employees can appeal if decisions made by the CEO are deemed inappropriate. The CEO should be willing to listen to the advisors and prayerfully submit to decisions that he may not agree with. However, it is up to the CEO to determine whether the recommendation will be binding for him because he is the one ultimately responsible. In order to be an effective leader, the CEO should not look at himself as the sole decision-maker in his company. He should seek counsel from others and confirm his decisions with others to assure he is not mislead by his own self-interests or the deceit of his own heart.

Authority in Government

God used government authority in the lives of many people in the Bible to accomplish His purposes in their life. Scripture tells us that even the king's heart is in the hand of God (See Proverbs 21:1). God uses these authorities to continue the work that He has started in us and will continue to manifest His character in us through governmental authorities. Moses and Pharaoh, Joseph and Potiphar, Daniel and Nebuchadnezzar, Esther and the king, Jesus and Pilate, and many others throughout the Bible became great men and women of God because they gave those in authority their rightful place.

> *Submit yourselves to every ordinance of man for the Lord's sake; whether it be the king, as supreme, or unto governors, as unto them that are sent by him for the punishment of evildoers, and for the praise of them that do well.*
>
> (1 Peter 2:13, 14 See also Romans 13:1;13:3,4-7)

God has established authority structures. If we find it difficult to live under the authorities in our life, we'll usually find it difficult to submit to the will of God in our lives too. Rebellion is reflected in our unwillingness to live under the authority placed over us. We may not have respect for the person who is the President of the United States, but we are still to honor and respect the position the presidency represents, and we are to recognize that God has placed him in authority over us. As long as we are not asked to violate a Biblical commandment, we must recognize those in authority as a God-given and that He is going to work through them on our behalf.

We cannot obey government when it calls us to compromise God's Word. The abortion issue and many other moral issues often times come into question. Each person must evaluate these situations in light of what God's Word says and be true to their own conscience.

Authority in the Church

Now we ask you, brothers, to respect those who work hard among you, who are over you in the Lord and who admonish you. Hold them in the highest regard in love because of their work. Live in peace with each other. (1 Thessalonians 5:13
See also Hebrews 13:7; 1 Timothy 5:17; 1 Peter 5:1-3)

The fourth area that God uses authority in is the church. God leads us by placing leaders within the church to provide direction for the church as a whole and us individually. We are encouraged to submit ourselves to their leadership and to pray for them. Church leaders must also have authority structures in place to insure they lead the church rightly in the ways of God. A pastor must have accountability as well as the elders.

Leaders in a local church body are held responsible for your spiritual condition. If they are not taking this responsibility serious before God, they are in danger of judgment by God. At the same time, you and I are responsible for submitting to their leadership in a joyful and willing manner. This should not be construed as lording over another person, but through servant leadership we follow just as the sheep follow the shepherd. I value greatly the input I gain from my pastor and other mentors that have played this role in my life. I believe God uses them to give me insight into areas that I may need light shed upon from time to time. If you are not in a church which functions in this way, I encourage you to become involved in such a church. If you cannot fully support the leader in your local fellowship, you should not be there unless God has specifically directed you to be there for some other reason. This would not be the case in most instances.

Reflection

1. How do you view those in authority over you? Can you appreciate them, or do you resent them? Explain.

2. Give an example of a time you had to give deference to someone in authority over you that was difficult.

3. Can you see that authority structures are there for protection, not for limiting our freedom?

7

Other Ways God Speaks to Us

Godly Principle:
God speaks through circumstances and other situations to give us direction.

Circumstances

God will often use circumstances in our lives to direct us in making and confirming our decisions. I have often discovered this to be the case after a situation has occurred and I can look back and see how it developed.

One such occasion involved a decision that I made as a result of a simple request. I had just launched a magazine designed for Christians in the workplace. I was having lunch with Larry Burkett who has done a great deal of writing and training in the area of Christians in the workplace. I had noticed that there were many grassroots marketplace organizations cropping up all over the country. I asked Larry if he was familiar with some of the groups. He was not. He then asked, "It would be nice to know what all these groups are doing so we don't duplicate efforts. Do you think you could invite some of these groups for a roundtable discussion?" I told him I would and proceeded to send a fax invitation to about four main marketplace ministries I had worked with in the workplace. A strange thing happened after I did that. I began to get requests from ministries all around the country that heard about the gathering who asked if they could come. By the time it was all over, 54 people showed up representing 45 organizations from around the country. Unfortunately, Larry had a last minute conflict and was not able to attend. That was the beginning of Marketplace Leaders, the ministry I now am focused on full time. I often joke that God tricked me into starting this ministry; God confirmed His direction for me through circumstances He orchestrated.

When I first met my wife, I was impressed to do something rather strange. I decided I would send her a stone in a box with a scripture verse that described how God used stones in the Bible. I was going to send one anonymously once a month for six months from a company called Significant Moments. The final month I planned to send the last stone with a note revealing who they were from that said, "The most significant moment was the day I met you." However, before this could happen, my plan was spoiled.

I was helping my wife (just a friend at the time) move her furniture. (I had just washed the stones that morning.) We were exchanging stories about our lives. She began to tell me the story of how she got her name. Her father was an orphan in England, and in England they give orphans different names from their given names. They named her father after a town in England called "Staines." Staines means "place of stones." She also shared with me that her father later learned that his real name was Malcolm Stones. I nearly drove off the road when she told me this story. My plan was foiled! But my faith was advanced light years. I told her about my plan since it would be too obvious now. We both looked at each other in amazement.

Ostrich

Another humorous circumstance God used to confirm direction involved my engagement to Angie. After we were engaged, a close friend had a wedding shower for her. Her friend CG came to the shower and said, "I have a gift for you and a gift for your future husband. My husband was very upset with me for giving him such a gift, but I was so impressed to give him this that I had to do it." Angie opened the gift bag and pulled out a beanie baby Ostrich.

Angie burst out laughing! "I cannot believe this! My pet name for Os is 'Ostrich'"!

Hosea 2

I've mentioned some instances in which God helped confirm my decision to marry Angie. Early in our relationship we began to see God's confirming hand to our relationship. In our second meeting together we were sharing our personal testimonies with one another. I had written a book on adversity that I brought to give her. In the front of the book I always signed my name with the scripture passage Hosea 2:14-20. These verses are passages that God uses to speak to me regarding the process He took me through in my spiritual journey. Before I gave Angie the book she began sharing her testimony with me and said that a particular passage of scripture was very meaningful to her. She then began quoting Hosea 2. I could hardly believe my ears. How many people do you know quote from Hosea 2 their primary scriptures that have led their lives?

God did many things like that over the course of nine months to help Angie and me see His hand in our relationship. These occurrences were confirmations of something we had sensed already.

Faithfulness To Convict

God can use circumstances to convict us of sin that may be keeping us from victory in our daily walks. Sin can prevent us from making Godly decisions in our life. I had recently come back from a mountaintop experience. As I attempted to get back into my routine, I found a great cloud of oppression come over me. Each day I attempted to press through it, but with no success. Fear, anxiety, doubt, and unbelief were setting in. I knew I was fretting over my future. I had been in a long period of transition in my business life and was tired of being in a place of waiting, yet didn't understand the oppression. It was definitely spiritual warfare.

That night I was reading a book by Os Guiness regarding our calling from God. (I should have figured something was up with a name like that!) He made mention that we can become envious of others when we get into a place where we are dissatisfied. Suddenly, I realized I was guilty of envying where other business people were in their lives. I was "subconsciously" angry that the calling God had placed on my life had involved so much adversity. I had to repent.

As if that were not enough, the next day the Holy Spirit confirmed my assessment in the most unusual way. That morning I turned on my computer to read my own Marketplace Meditation that is sent to my computer. The message was on "Envying Others" and included the same scripture reference that Guiness used in his book. Imagine God using my own words to convict me of sin! To make matters worse, at lunchtime I tuned into the local Christian radio station to hear an interview with Os Guiness just as he cited the very passage I had read the day before. I was shocked to realize how the Holy Spirit could be so precise in His ability to convict and give proof of His activity in my life.

Casting Lots

The Priest and the Tabernacle

Also put the Urim and the Thummim in the breastpiece, so they may be over Aaron's heart whenever he enters the presence of the LORD. Thus Aaron will always bear the means of making decisions for the Israelites over his heart before the Lord.
(Exodus 28:30)

In Exodus we find that God gave specific instructions to the priests for entering the tabernacle. They were to wear a breastplate that had jewels, which represented each of the twelve tribes. The breastpiece was a square piece of cloth folded in half upward to form a sort of pouch in a nine-inch-by-nine inch square. No one really knows what Urim or Thummin is. All we know is that they were often used in times of crisis to determine the will of God, but just how they functioned and what they looked like is unknown. They were designed to help determine decisions based on "if this happens, then this is the decision. If the other happens, then that is the decision." It is much like the flip of a coin, or the casting of lots. It was not up to the priest to determine the final decision. God was to determine that. The urim and thummim were what God used to take the decision away from the priest and leave it with Himself. We are each stewards over what God has placed in our care, but not necessarily the ones to make the final decisions. God reserves the right for that.

I fully expect I will lose some readers as I seek to present casting of lots as a possible means of making decisions, yet, we see in scripture, both in the Old Testament and the New Testament where it was used to decide a matter. After all, it seems like it is nothing less than gambling with a decision and leaving it to chance. How could one simplify a decision to the flipping of a coin, which is exactly what casting a lot is? Is that really the case? I believe what is really at the heart of this is a willingness to release control of a decision to the Lord, which is what Proverbs says.

> *The lot is cast into the lap, but its every decision is from the LORD.*

(Proverbs 16:33)

It appears to me that the casting of lots was used more or less as a tiebreaker. If two people don't have a clear direction, or there is a dispute, then both are willing to yield their decision and let the lot determine the outcome. This takes the control away from each person. It does not appear that it was used as an ongoing means of direction and decision-making, except in the case of the priests with the urim and thummim.

When the disciples had to replace Judas, they chose two men as possible replacements. You would have thought they would have prayed and fasted until they got the answer, or they simply could have taken a vote. They didn't do either of these; they cast lots to make the final choice. They obviously believed in the early Hebraic principle of casting a lot to make a final decision.

> *So they proposed two men: Joseph called Barsabbas (also known as Justus) and Matthias. Then they prayed, "Lord, you know everyone's heart. Show us which of these two you have chosen to take over this apostolic ministry, which Judas left to go*

where he belongs." Then they cast lots, and the lot fell to Matthias; so he was added to the eleven apostles. (Acts 1:23-26)

Once when Zechariah's division was on duty and he was serving as priest before God, he was chosen by lot, according to the custom of the priesthood, to go into the temple of the Lord and burn incense. (Luke 1:8-10)

What might be a practical application of this principle? In the early church casting lots was an effective means of finalizing a matter to avoid disputes.

Casting the lot settles disputes and keeps strong opponents apart. (Proverbs 18:18)

The next time you have a disagreement with your spouse or someone else and you find yourself at an impasse, ask them if the decision can be determined by flipping a coin. This may not appear to be very spiritual, but if it was good enough for the disciples, it should be good enough for us. Granted, all the other means listed in this study are the preferred ways of working toward a decision, but this age-old principle still has merit in some applications. This method allows the decision to rest in the Lord's hand. More importantly it will really tell you who wants control versus who wants the will of God in the matter. Again, let me emphasize that I believe our first course of action should always be to seek the mind of God and allow the Holy Spirit to direct our steps.

Reflection

1. Have you ever experienced a time when you felt God gave you direction through a circumstance?

2. What precautions might you undertake when considering a circumstance as confirming a decision?

3. Can you think of situations when casting a lot (or flipping a coin or drawing straws) might have been appropriate to settle a dispute?

8

Presumption versus Faith

Decision Principle:
Understanding the difference between Biblical faith and presumption
will keep us from making wrong decisions.

Moving in presumption can be a source of poor decisions. It is important to understand a distinction between Biblical faith and presumption. There are two kinds of presumption that we want to discuss in this chapter. The first kind is when we think we're acting out of obedience, when in reality it is only half-hearted obedience that often violates Biblical principles. The second kind is when we make decisions based on what we believe is faith, when in actuality it is something we have conjured up in our own minds.

God has given us several examples in scripture when his servants moved beyond faith into presumption. Let us look at some and see how they might apply to us.

Uzzah and the Ark

Make poles of acacia wood for the altar and overlay them with bronze. The poles
are to be inserted into the rings so they will be on two sides of the altar when it is
carried. Make the altar hollow, out of boards. It is to be made just as you were
shown on the mountain. (Exodus 27:6-8)

David's men were transporting the ark of the covenant. He had been given strict instructions about how to transport the ark. It was to be carried using poles. It was not to be touched or moved on a cart. However, David did not seem to think this was important and made some assumptions that cost him the life of one of his most trusted men.

They set the ark of God on a new cart and brought it from the house of Abinadab,
which was on the hill. Uzzah and Ahio, sons of Abinadab, were guiding the new
cart with the ark of God on it, and Ahio was walking in front of it. David and the
whole house of Israel were celebrating with all their might before the LORD, with
songs and with harps, lyres, tambourines, sistrums and cymbals. When they came
to the threshing floor of Nacon, Uzzah reached out and took hold of the ark of God,
because the oxen stumbled. The LORD's anger burned against Uzzah because of his
irreverent act; therefore God struck him down and he died there beside the ark of
God. Then David was angry because the LORD's wrath had broken out against
Uzzah, and to this day that place is called Perez Uzzah.   (2 Samuel 6:3-8)

Uzzah moved in presumption. You and I can make the same mistake. When we
don't whole-heartedly follow God's principles, our decisions will result in failure. Often
I hear business people questioning why God does not bless their endeavor. After further investigation, I discover that they have violated a basic Biblical principle. God, who
is righteous and just, cannot violate His Word, no matter what. Before you make a
decision and take action, make sure you're not violating a Biblical principle in any way.

Moses Strikes the Rock

Moses was leading the Israelites through the desert. It was a trying time for him. The
people were grumbling. They were thirsty and needed water to drink. Moses sought
the Lord for wisdom. God gave Moses the answer—to simply speak to the rock and it
would bring forth water.

Take the staff, and you and your brother Aaron gather the assembly together. Speak
to that rock before their eyes and it will pour out its water.   (Numbers 20:7-8)

Moses was to use his words, instead of his staff to bring forth another miracle.
Instead, Moses became infuriated with the people and lost his temper. Moses made a
strategic error that ultimately cost him his inheritance to enter the Promised Land.

So Moses took the staff from the LORD's presence, just as he commanded him. He
and Aaron gathered the assembly together in front of the rock and Moses said to
them, "Listen, you rebels, must we bring you water out of this rock?" Then Moses
raised his arm and struck the rock twice with his staff. Water gushed out, and the
community and their livestock drank. But the LORD said to Moses and Aaron,
"Because you did not trust in me enough to honor me as holy in the sight of the
Israelites, you will not bring this community into the land I give them."

(Numbers 20:9-12)

Moses presumed that he could represent God in a fashion that was not pleasing to Him and get away with it. It is interesting that God still allowed Moses to still perform the miracle, in spite of his disobedience. God's grace so often covers our imperfections in spite of ourselves. This is a testimony of His grace in our lives. However, sin always comes with a price, and because this was not a one-time occurrence with Moses, God finally judged him with what appears to be a harsh judgment: not allowing him to enter the Promised Land. However, when we look at this situation, we find that God had been patient with him for a very long time. Moses' anger had been a continual problem that went back as far as the day he struck the Egyptian.

There are sins that you and I have in our lives that can keep each of us from receiving our spiritual and physical inheritance if we continue to walk in disobedience. There is a point where God says "enough is enough." Once we reach that point, we've lost something tangible that God wanted to give us. Ask God to show you if there is any sin that you are still harboring. You must not presume that you can continue to harbor sin and expect God to bless your life.

Presumptive Faith

There is a particular teaching that is prominent today in some circles of the church that says that faith comes by believing and that we can generate more faith if we try harder or meditate and repeat scripture verses. It is a teaching that appeals especially to the more developed nations in which prosperity is tied to the physical blessing of God. There are physical and financial blessings from God, but there are also seasons in our life in which physical and material blessings may not be realized. Joseph was described as being blessed when he was a servant in Pharoah's household and during his prison experience. Most Christians today would hardly describe blessing in those terms. My English friend, Peter Michell, in his book *Faith or Presumption*, gives us further insights into the problem with this teaching.

> We see many make a "stand" on what they consider the written Word of God to say, only to be bitterly disappointed. To assume that the Lord will give you the answer you demand, based on your use and interpretation of scripture is a misunderstanding of faith. Faith comes from the little phrase or saying proceeding from the mouth of God now. The Lord wants a living relationship with each of His children, a relationship of communication. That is why prayer is such an important thing. The Lord wants to hear from us! Also, He wants us to hear from Him. Meditating on the written Word produces hope—that produces faith in the sense of trust. Miracle working, mountain-moving faith comes only by hearing God for yourself for the

specific situation.

Many who have gone down this path of teaching find themselves disappointed and discouraged, concluding that they must not have enough faith. This brings condemnation and in many cases leaves the believer in a hopeless state in their Christian walk. The problem is that there is a lot of truth mixed in with an unbalanced view of what the scriptures really teach regarding faith. We cannot force God into action. He is not a puppet that must respond just because we have followed a formula to build faith. It is clear from New Testament scriptures that not everyone was healed when they prayed. Paul had an eye problem that was not healed (Galatians 4:15). He became sick in Tromphimus sick in Miletum (2 Timothy 4:20) and he told Timothy to take wine for his stomach problem (1 Timothy 5:23). Certainly Paul could have appropriated enough faith to "believe for his healing" had this been the way to appropriate faith. We must realize healing and other manifestations are a result of faith combined with grace, with grace being the more important element.[3]

This is why confirmation from different sources is important in the process of determining God's will in a matter. What is the balance between these two principles we have just described? Let me give you an example.

A Miracle at a Plastics Manufacturer

He replied, "Because you have so little faith. I tell you the truth, if you have faith as small as a mustard seed, you can say to this mountain, 'Move from here to there' and it will move. Nothing will be impossible for you."   (Matthew 17:20)

Gunnar Olson, the Swedish founder of the International Christian Chamber of Commerce, tells a story about God performing a miracle in his own business a few years ago. He owns a plastics company in Sweden. They make huge plastic bags that are used to cover bales of hay in the farmlands across Europe. It was the harvest season and they were getting ready to ship thousands of pallets of these bags to their customers. More than 1,000 pallets were ready to ship when an alarming discovery was made. Every bag on the warehouse floor had sealed shut from top to bottom. Scientists declared the entire stock as worthless trash. Nothing could be done. The company would go out of business. Gunnar, his wife, and children sought the Lord in prayer about this catastrophe. The Holy Spirit spoke through various family members.

The wife said, "If God can turn water into wine, what are plastics?"

The daughter said, "I don't believe this is from the Lord. We should stand against it."

Gunnar sensed they were to trust God for a miracle in this situation. They continued to pray. They took authority over this mountain of a problem based on Matthew 17, which gave them the authority to cast a mountain into the sea if faith only the size of a mustard seed could be exercised. The following Sunday they went to the warehouse and laid hands on every pallet asking the Lord to restore the bags to their original condition. It took several hours. The next day, the employees began to inspect the bags. As they inspected the bags, they discovered that every single bag had been restored to its original condition; an incredible miracle had taken place!

What were the steps they followed in the process? First, Gunnar went home and shared the problem with his family. Together, they prayed and God spoke to each family member about the situation. He confirmed the steps through each person as to what should be done. They exercised their faith in the *rhema* Word they received from God. The result was a miracle. This is how Biblical faith should work.

A Book Testimony

I was going through a major transition in my work life. I was now doing more writing and less consulting. We had received a major shipment of my most recent book from our publisher. We had 24 boxes of them in our basement. One day I was thinking about the principle of the widow and her oil that is described in 1 Kings 17 and the principle of speaking to the situation (see Matthew 17). One of the principles of provision is that God often provides through what is already in our hand. I felt impressed that Angie and I should go down to our basement, lay hands on our boxes of books and speak over them a mustard seed prayer of faith that encourages us to speak to the mountain as mentioned in the previous story. When I mentioned this to Angie, she said she had been thinking the same thing. I stood over the books and prayed, "Lord, you know these books do little good in this basement. In Jesus' name we ask you to move these books out of here and into the hands of those who will be blessed by them!" Three hours later I received a call from a marketplace ministry. They ordered thirteen boxes of books—the largest single order we had ever had!

Reflection

1. Are there any areas in your life in which you are presuming God will bless you when you know there is sin that exist in your life? Confess any sin that may be keeping you from being blessed by God.

2. Can you think of an example of presumption in your on life in which you failed because you presumed upon God by moving ahead of Him?

3. What is the key lesson you can learn from this teaching on presumption and faith?

9

Confirming Decisions

Godly Decision Principle:
Once you make a decision, seek confirmation.

Now that we have established some guidelines for making decisions, we need to discuss ways to confirm them. There are times when we must make quick decisions during the course of a day and we need to have the freedom to use our God-given wisdom to make those decisions. God speaks through many different ways and as we become one with Him, we become more integrated in our ability to move and be led by the Holy Spirit (Romans 8:14). The scriptures do not indicate that God was constantly communicating moment by moment with His people. However, God does encourage us to seek Him moment by moment in our lives. Not every decision we must make can afford, nor is it necessary, to be confirmed. Jesus encourages us to abide in the vine, which means we should be walking in close fellowship with Him and know that He is guiding us throughout our day. However, the scriptures also convey a principle of confirmation that can greatly reduce the frequency of making poor decisions. Therefore, I would highly recommend that any major decision be confirmed through a few different sources.

F. B. Meyer's Formula

One night as the famous Bible teacher F.B. Meyer stood on the deck of a ship approaching land, he wondered how the crew knew when and how to safely steer to the dock. It was a stormy night, and visibility was low. Meyer, standing on the bridge and peering through the window, asked "Captain, how do you know when to turn this ship into that narrow harbor?"

"That's an art," replied the captain. "Do you see those three red lights on the shore? When they're all in a straight line I go right in!"

Later Meyer said: "When we want to know God's will, there are three things which always occur: the inward impulse, the Word of God, and the trend of circumstances. Never act until these three things agree."[4]

The Role of Spouses in Making Decisions

When John Benson decided to make some financial investments in a new business venture, he was very excited about the possibilities for a handsome financial return. His business and financial background had served him well. John felt strongly that his wife Jenny would not understand the complexity of his investment, so he casually mentioned it to her. When she asked a few simple questions, John became defensive and justified his investing in the venture. Jenny felt uneasy about the investment, but since he had been so successful in the past, she laid aside her reservations and left the responsibility up to John. A year later, after investing a large sum of money, John received a phone call from the investment company. It seems that the principals of the company had fled the country and were not to be found. All the investors who had put money in the company were going to lose their investment with no ability to recoup it. Many astute investors had been taken in on the scam.

This story could be retold repeatedly across the world. God's principles for making decisions require input from both spouses, regardless of their level of expertise. I learned this lesson the hard way after making many independent decisions outside the counsel of my wife. Today, whenever I am faced with a major decision, I first consult the Lord, and then I consult my wife. She may disagree totally with something that seems very straightforward to me, but I have learned not to move forward if she is not in agreement. She does not need to know all the details, nor does she have to have expertise. God has placed in her a "chip" called "intuition." That intuition cannot explain why she feels the way she does, she just knows when something is not right. Conversely, husbands bring a totally different perspective that may give an alternative side to a situation that the wife has never considered. God has called married couples to be one. If we seek to make decisions independently, then we are benefiting from only 50% of the intended resource God has placed within our grasp. In marriage, this stewardship of decisions requires two people. God blesses this union by honoring the decisions made with the motive of glorifying God and relying on His Spirit to lead in our decision-making process.

Confirmation Through Others

The scriptures encourage us to seek advice and counsel from others. This counsel needs to be from other Godly people who share the same values and goals that we have.

Plans fail for lack of counsel, but with many advisers they succeed.

(Proverbs 15:22)

The way of a fool seems right to him, but a wise man listens to advice.

(Proverbs 12:15)

Pride only breeds quarrels, but wisdom is found in those who take advice.

(Proverbs 13:10)

Listen to advice and accept instruction, and in the end you will be wise.

(Proverbs 19:20)

Make plans by seeking advice; if you wage war, obtain guidance.

(Proverbs 20:18)

Keeping A Balance With Counsel From Others

We should strive to maintain balance when seeking input from others and making decisions as we feel God is leading. This process is designed to confirm direction for which we are seeking confirmation. Paul was sensitive to getting too heavy-handed in the confirmation process. He offered advice but was not the enforcer of someone's decision.

And here is my advice about what is best for you in this matter.

(2 Corinthians 8:10)

There is a principle of agreement among two or three individuals throughout the scriptures to confirm a decision, but even this does not negate a person's right to make independent decisions. The requirement for efficient administration frequently requires single points of decision-making. Where there is willingness and trust to receive input, there is probably also humility, faith, and grace for God to work His pleasure in His servant. Where there is unwillingness, the opposite is true.

There have been times in my life where I have felt strongly about a certain issue only to receive feedback from those close to me which revealed that I was not accurate in my assessment of the situation. I have learned to yield in such situations, trusting that God is working through those in whom I am accountable.

Peace of Mind

Peace of mind is another important confirmation for decisions. If you do not have peace about a decision, you should wait until God gives you peace. This does not mean your decision may not have some tension due to the faith aspect of it, but deep down you should have a peace that it is the right decision.

Do not be anxious about anything, but in everything, by prayer and petition, with thanksgiving, present your requests to God. And the peace of God, which transcends all understanding, will guard your hearts and your minds in Christ Jesus.

(Philippians 4:6-7)

Reflection

1. Why is seeking confirmation a good idea before proceeding with a decision?

2. Why do you believe having agreement with your spouse a good idea?

3. What do you believe God's motivation is behind encouraging counsel from others for making decisions?

10

Timing for Implementing Decisions

Godly Decision Principle:
Once you make a decision that requires action, make sure you carry out
the action on God's timetable, not your own.

There is a time for everything, and a season for every activity under heaven:
A time to be born and a time to die, a time to plant and a time to uproot,
A time to kill and a time to heal, a time to tear down and a time to build,
A time to weep and a time to laugh, a time to mourn and a time to dance,
A time to scatter stones and a time to gather them, a time to embrace and a time to
refrain, a time to search and a time to give up, a time to keep and a time to throw
away, a time to tear and a time to mend, a time to be silent and a time to speak, a
time to love and a time to hate, a time for war and a time for peace What does the
worker gain from his toil? I have seen the burden God has laid on men. He has
made everything beautiful in its time. (Ecclesiastes 3:1-11)

Now that we have determined the various methods for making and confirming decisions, it's important to discuss the timing of implementing or carrying out decisions. Once we make a decision, it does not necessarily mean we are to take action right away. Jesus often spoke to the disciples about not telling others about a miracle He performed, citing that it was not the right time for others to know about Him. There are many examples of making a decision and then waiting on God's time for implementation.

Earlier I gave the example of David and the balsam trees and how he had learned to constantly seek God for direction. The second time the Philistines were planning to attack him, he asked God if he should attack just as he did before. God told him that he was to attack, but not until he heard the marching in the balsam trees. Timing was important to the execution of the direction God gave him, which was to attack only when he heard the marching in the balsam trees.

When God told Moses that He would deliver the Israelites from slavery through Moses' hand, Moses did not realize it was going to take so many different plagues before they would finally be freed. Even though God warned him ahead of time, Moses never quite realized the tremendous resistance Pharoah would display in the process. It became a source of frustration for Moses, but the timing of release was important to make sure that the glory of God was revealed through Moses and God's mighty acts. When Moses finally led them out of Egypt to the Red Sea, God did not immediately open the Red Sea to them. It was only after the Egyptian army was at their door. God waited until the time was right.

I learned from personal experience that some of my decisions were from God, but the timing to implement was not. When God led me to begin writing about some of my experiences, He also revealed to me that I was to be involved in publishing. I recall being awakened early one morning with a burden on my heart to publish books. Months later, I began a publishing company. We published four books and a magazine, but through a series of negative events and a lack of investment capital, I was unable to publish anything else. The company lay dormant for three years. I concluded that I had jumped ahead of the Lord in the timing of the venture. In spite of my losses, the burden to publish remained in my heart. During that time an intercessor gave me a word during our prayer time that what had died would be resurrected, but it "would almost seem insignificant in my eyes." It was that month that I began writing a daily e-mail devotional for workplace Christians that is now circulated throughout the world. However, the issue of publishing the books I had in my heart was still unresolved.

Every week I would complain to Angie about what was in my heart about publishing. I placed manuscripts with other publishing firms, only to have them say after waiting months for their decision that they had decided not to publish me. Angie did not have peace about taking out a loan to start a new publishing venture. She didn't want to go into more debt. I am by nature a risk taker, but I had learned by this time not to do anything if my wife was not in total agreement. Thus, I waited and waited for what seemed an eternity. One day, after one of my complaining moments about publishing, Angie asked me if I had finished the devotional book I was working on. When I said, "No," she said, "When you finish the book, God is going to give you a publisher." Like most husbands I know, I discounted the comment and walked off in frustration. A couple of months later, I met with the president and acquisitions editor of a publishing company from the northeast. I shared my testimony with them, and after our time together they offered to not only publish the devotional book, but also another one I had been working on. That turned out to be the day I finished devotional number 365, the day I finished the book Angie had asked me about!

A few months later, a subscriber to my devotionals called to say how much they meant to him. It just so happened he was also the acquisitions editor for another major publishing firm. He asked if I would consider writing three small books for their company. Within three months I now had contracts to write five books in one year and guaranteed distribution in the largest Christian bookstore chain in the nation.

After I began to write, I was in desperate need of an editor. I couldn't afford to hire an editor. One day an English teacher in Japan responded to one of my devotionals over the internet. He suggested that I get someone to look over my work, as it was often not as grammatically correct as it should be. (This was a risk I decided to take when I began writing the devotional, knowing my grammar wasn't that great. It was a faith decision.) When I responded to this man's comment, I asked if he would be interested in assisting me. He agreed and has become the editor for my work—all the way from Japan—and for free!

I have learned that if God places something in our heart, He will also bring it to pass (1 Thessalonians 5:24). However, His timing is just as important as the initial message He gives us. We must wait for His timing and gain confirmation from those close to us and to whom we are accountable. Another thing to remember is when God's initiatives direct in our lives we don't always know what the end-product will look like. I could have never imagined getting into publishing in the way that He brought it about. His ways are truly not our ways.

> For my thoughts are not your thoughts, neither are your ways my ways, declares
> the LORD. As the heavens are higher than the earth, so are my ways higher than
> your ways and my thoughts than your thoughts. (Isaiah 55:8-9)

In my journey, I often wondered why there were so many delays in my situation to fulfill what I knew God had spoken about my life. Part of the reason was that God wanted to develop more character qualities that the waiting time was designed to do. Another reason was that God is often putting other players in place that will be part of our process that are only to come onto the scene at a certain time. All of these factors play a role in waiting on God's timing to move upon a decision.

You should give the same level of consideration to the timing of the implementation of the decision as to making the decision itself. Ask God to confirm the time for implementing the decision once you've made it.

> *Then the LORD replied: "Write down the revelation and make it plain on tablets so that a herald may run with it. For the revelation awaits an appointed time; it speaks of the end and will not prove false. Though it linger, wait for it; it will certainly come and will not delay."* (Habakkuk 2:2-3)

Reflection

1. Why do you think it is important to determine the timing and implementation of a decision?

2. Based on the above, what is the best way to insure that you will act in God's timing and not your own?

3. Can you think of examples of decisions you have made but the timing to move on the decision was not quite right?

Conclusion

...because those who are led by the Spirit of God are sons of God.   (Romans 8:14)

Following God's method of decision-making and confirmation can significantly reduce making wrong decisions in life and work. Most of us have the problem of really desiring to leave these decisions to God. If we are to move in the power of the Holy Spirit in our lives and experience the peace and assurance of God working in and through us, we must follow God's ways in this important area. Our society and even the church today often avoid the kind of involvement and accountability that God calls for in His body today. I pray that you will follow God's ways of making decisions so that He is glorified and manifested in your life.

A Final Thought

On autumn nights as we sleep peacefully in our beds, millions of songbirds are quietly traveling under cover of darkness, heading south for warmer climates. Take Baltimore orioles, for example. Every fall, they pack their bags, close up their homes, leaving the key under the mat, and like senior citizens head south. It's the weather patterns that tell the birds that it is time to move. "As cold fronts move across eastern North America," wrote one expert, "they're sending waves of orioles, along gorges in Mexico and Latin America." As cold fronts pass, clear skies and north winds usually follow. These conditions are ideal for migration, allowing the birds to travel with no risk of storms, the wind at their backs and a clear view of the stars to help them find their way.

They fly over thousands of houses and highways, shopping centers and parking lots, passing state after state. If a particular oriole opts for a direct flight home, it will fly over the Gulf of Mexico in a single night, crossing six hundred miles of open water.

The entire trip from Baltimore to Mexico, Panama, or Costa Rica takes about two weeks, but the oriole knows exactly where it is going. God planted within its little brain a perfect guidance system that tells it exactly where to go, and when, and how.

The Bible says that we are more valuable to the Lord than all the birds in the sky. We are worth more than many sparrows. If the Lord is pleased to guide the birds in their migrations, it's a safe bet that He also wants to guide our lives.[5]

Notes

1. Henry Blackaby, Claude King, *Experiencing God*, Lifeway Press, Nashville, TN, p. 33-34

2. J. Oswald Sanders, "Lessons I've Learned," *Discipleship Journal*, Issue 15, 1983, p. 14.

3. Peter Michell, *Faith or Presumption*, ICCC, Fleet, Hampshire, UK, 1998, p. 31

4. Robert J. Morgan, *Stories, Illustrations and Quotes*, Thomas Nelson Publishers, Nashville, TN, 2000, p. 369

5. Robert J. Morgan, *Stories, Illustrations and Quotes*, Thomas Nelson Publishers, Nashville, TN, 2000, p. 372

Marketplace Leaders

Marketplace Leader's purpose is to raise up and train men and women to fulfill their calling in and through the workplace and to view their work as their ministry.

Our primary means of accomplishing this is through four key focuses.

1. Building Unity (John 17:23) –

Marketplace Leader Summits are held to encourage unity among marketplace ministries serving men and women in the workplace.

Our *Marketplace Resource Connection* is a monthly e-mail bulletin for marketplace ministries to inform and communicate the various services and activities of marketplace ministries. Our website also features many articles and resources.

2. Training New Leaders

Our workshops are designed to raise up and encourage men and women through mentoring and training programs.

Called to the Workplace–From Esau to Joseph one-day workshops are designed to help Christians understand their calling in the workplace.

TGIF Today God Is First marketplace meditations is a free daily e-mail devotional that encourages you to put God first in the workplace. It is distributed via the internet to thousands daily around the world. (visit our website to subscribe.)

MarketplaceRhema is a monthly teaching newsletter that features indepth articles on faith and work distributed by e-mail.

3. Publishing

Marketplace Leaders develops new resources targeted for Christians in business including *Called to the Workplace – Esau to Joseph* audio tape/workbook and an *Online Catalog* of resources specifically selected for workplace Christians.

4. Consulting

Marketplace Leaders provides marketing consulting to organizations to help them in the development of their companies from a Biblical perspective. Strategic planning, marketing, and creative communications are services we provide.

Let us know how we can assist you in furthering your organization. Call Os Hillman at 770-442-1500 or contact him via e-mail at os@marketplaceleaders.org.

Marketplace Leaders
3595 Webb Bridge Road
Alpharetta, GA 30005-4140 USA

Telephone: 770-442-1500
Fax: 770-442-1844

E-mail: os@marketplaceleaders.org
Web site: www.marketplaceleaders.org

Other Resources by Os Hillman

TGIF Today God Is First
365 Meditations on the Principles of Christ in the Workplace
hardback

It began as a series of daily e-mail meditations for his business associates. Today, it is one of the fastest growing devotionals on the internet and is now a book of 365 daily meditations especially geared for men and women in the workplace. Os has the uncanny ability to write just to people's circumstances to help men and women understand how to walk with God in the everyday trials of life.

The Purposes of Money
Exposing the Five Fallacies About Money
and God's Five Purposes for Its Use
softcover

One day a series of crises entered the world of this successful advertising agency executive that would alter his life forever. These life-changing events led him to discover wrong priorities and how may business people have erroneously viewed money. Questions for reflection at the end of each section make this 48-page booklet excellent for individual and group study.

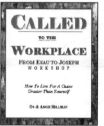

Called to the Workplace: From Esau to Joseph
How To Live For A Cause Greater Than Yourself
audio tape series, $95.00

Called to the Workplace: From Esau to Joseph is a six-tape audio series with workbook that is Os Hillman's complete one-day workshop. This workshop helps men and women discover their purpose in work and life. This workshop is loaded with practical application principles to understand God's method of calling, Biblical decision-making, and the role adversity plays in every believers life. *(Not available in stores. See our website to order.)*

Faith & Work: Do They Mix?
Discovering God's Purposes for Your Work
softcover

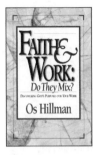

When you go to work on Monday, do you take your faith with you? Hillman provides Biblical insight into God's view of work and how our faith should be integrated into all aspects of life. Hillman's practical examples from scripture and his own story will encourage you in your journey to find purpose and meaning in your work life.

Adversity & Pain: The Gifts Nobody Wants
Discover God's Purposes for Adversity in our Lives.
softcover

"Hillman's vulnerability in relating his own suffering adds a personal and compassionate tone to a thorough presentation of the purpose and usefulness of pain in Christian's lives. Hillman's recurring theme is that God is GOD, and His reign over our lives isn't intended to be a democracy."

–Kris Wilson, March 1997 *CBA Marketplace Magazine Review*

Proven Strategies for Business Success
20 Years of Marketing Wisdom
softcover

Os Hillman has helped some of the America's leading small and large companies become better marketers. As an owner of an advertising agency for more than 13 years, Hillman has helped companies develop 24 proven strategies for business success. Presented in a 70-page booklet, it contains his 20 years of wisdom on subjects related to marketing and advertising in bite-size chapters. (*Not available in stores. See our website to order.*)

Available from your local Family Christian Bookstores

Marketplace Leaders
3595 Webb Bridge Road, Alpharetta, GA 30005-4140 USA
Telephone: 770-442-1500 Fax: 770-442-1844
www.marketplaceleaders.org

NOTES

NOTES